Lorraine Ann

Journal

BARBOUR
PUBLISHING

Pure and Lovely
ISBN 978-1-60260-888-7
With the Heart
ISBN 978-1-60260-889-4

All scripture quotations are taken from the King James Version
of the Bible.

Published by Barbour Publishing, Inc., P.O. Box 719,
Uhrichsville, OH 44683, www.barbourbooks.com

*Our mission is to publish and distribute inspirational products
offering exceptional value and biblical encouragement to the masses.*

Member of the
Evangelical Christian
Publishers Association

Printed in Thailand.

Be ye glad and rejoice for ever in that which I create: for, behold, I create Jerusalem a rejoicing, and her people a joy.
ISAIAH 65:18

_____

_____

_____

_____

_____

_____

_____

_____

_____

_____

_____

_____

_____

_____

_____

_____

_____

_____

_____

_____

Never lose an opportunity of seeing anything that is beautiful; for beauty is God's handwriting—a wayside sacrament. Welcome it in every fair face, in every fair sky, in every fair flower, and thank God for it as a cup of blessing.
RALPH WALDO EMERSON

We may run, walk, stumble. . .or fly, but let us never lose sight of the reason for the journey or miss a chance to see a rainbow on the way.

GLORIA GAITHER

_____

_____

_____

_____

_____

_____

_____

_____

_____

_____

_____

_____

_____

_____

_____

_____

_____

_____

_____

_____

Joy is the holy fire that keeps our purpose warm and our intelligence aglow. Work without joy shall be as nothing. Resolve to keep happy, and your joy and you shall form an invincible host against difficulties.
HELEN KELLER

Dreams are renewable. No matter what our age or condition, there are still untapped possibilities within us and new beauty waiting to be born.

DALE E. TURNER

_____

_____

_____

_____

_____

_____

_____

_____

_____

_____

_____

_____

_____

_____

_____

_____

_____

_____

*Laughter is the gift of love, the music of
the soul, and the essence of humanity.*
KELLY EILEEN HAKE

_____

_____

_____

_____

_____

_____

_____

_____

_____

_____

_____

_____

_____

_____

_____

_____

_____

_____

Destiny is not a matter of chance; it is a matter of choice.
It is not a thing to be waited for; it is a thing to be achieved.
WILLIAM JENNINGS BRYAN

> The future enters into us, in order to transform
> itself in us, long before it happens.
> RAINER MARIA RILKE

_____

_____

_____

_____

_____

_____

_____

_____

_____

_____

_____

_____

_____

_____

_____

_____

_____

_____

_____

The LORD hath done great things for us; whereof we are glad.
PSALM 126:3

He that is of a merry heart hath a continual feast.
PROVERBS 15:15

_____

_____

_____

_____

_____

_____

_____

_____

_____

_____

_____

_____

_____

_____

_____

_____

_____

_____

_____

_____

Beauty is the mark God sets on virtue. Every natural
action is graceful; every heroic act is also decent,
and causes the place and the bystanders to shine.

RALPH WALDO EMERSON

> *Use what talent you possess—the woods would be very silent if no birds sang except those that sang best.*
>
> HENRY VAN DYKE

_____

_____

_____

_____

_____

_____

_____

_____

_____

_____

_____

_____

_____

_____

_____

_____

_____

_____

Yesterday is gone. Tomorrow has not yet come.
We have only today. Let us begin.

MOTHER TERESA

> The eagle that soars in the upper air does
> not worry itself how it is to cross rivers.
> GLADYS AYLWARD

Life itself cannot give you joy unless you really will it.
Life just gives you time and space—it's up to you to fill it.
CHINESE PROVERB

*The greatest satisfaction in life is achieving
what everyone said could not be done.*
CHINESE PROVERB

_____

_____

_____

_____

_____

_____

_____

_____

_____

_____

_____

_____

_____

_____

_____

_____

_____

_____

_____

The journey of a thousand miles
must begin with a single step.
LAO TZU

The human heart has hidden treasures,
In secret kept, in silence sealed—
The thoughts, the hopes, the dreams, the pleasures,
Whose charms were broken if revealed.
CHARLOTTE BRONTË

_____

_____

_____

_____

_____

_____

_____

_____

_____

_____

_____

_____

_____

_____

_____

_____

_____

_____

The LORD is my shepherd; I shall not want.
PSALM 23:1

Be still, and know that I am God.
PSALM 46:10

_____

_____

_____

_____

_____

_____

_____

_____

_____

_____

_____

_____

_____

_____

_____

_____

_____

_____

The best things are nearest: breath in your nostrils, light in your eyes, flowers at your feet, duties at your hand, the path of God just before you.
ROBERT LOUIS STEVENSON

People grow through experience if they meet life honestly and courageously. This is how character is built.
ELEANOR ROOSEVELT

_____

_____

_____

_____

_____

_____

_____

_____

_____

_____

_____

_____

_____

_____

_____

_____

_____

_____

The purpose of life is a life of purpose.
ROBERT BYRNE

Your vision will become clear only when you look into your heart.
Who looks outside, dreams. Who looks inside, awakens.

CARL JUNG

_____

_____

_____

_____

_____

_____

_____

_____

_____

_____

_____

_____

_____

_____

_____

_____

_____

_____

_____

Always laugh when you can.
It is cheap medicine.
LORD BYRON

Little faith will bring your soul to heaven,
but great faith will bring heaven to your soul.

CHARLES H. SPURGEON

If you can imagine it, you can achieve it.
If you can dream it, you can become it.
WILLIAM ARTHUR WARD

*Life is what we are alive to. It is not length but breadth. . . .
Be alive to. . .goodness, kindness, purity, love, history,
poetry, music, flowers, stars, God, and eternal hope.*

MALTBIE D. BABCOCK

_____

_____

_____

_____

_____

_____

_____

_____

_____

_____

_____

_____

_____

_____

_____

_____

_____

_____

For, lo, the winter is past, the rain is over and gone; the flowers appear on the earth; the time of the singing of birds is come.

SONG OF SOLOMON 2:11–12

With my song will I praise him.
PSALM 28:7

_____
_____
_____
_____
_____
_____
_____
_____
_____
_____
_____
_____
_____
_____
_____
_____
_____
_____
_____

Rest is not idleness, and to lie sometimes on the grass under trees on a summer's day, listening to the murmur of the water or watching the clouds float across the sky, is by no means a waste of time.
SIR JOHN LUBBOCK

Take the first step in faith. You don't have to see the whole staircase, just take the first step.
MARTIN LUTHER KING JR.

_____

_____

_____

_____

_____

_____

_____

_____

_____

_____

_____

_____

_____

_____

_____

_____

_____

_____

_____

I will take time to notice the good things when they come.
I will fix my mind on what is pure and lovely and upright.
ANITA CORRINE DONIHUE

When I think upon my God, my heart is so full
of joy that the notes dance and leap from my pen.
JOSEPH HAYDN

Dream what you want to dream; go where you want to go; be what you want to be, because you have only one life and one chance to do all the things you want to do.

_____

_____

_____

_____

_____

_____

_____

_____

_____

_____

_____

_____

_____

_____

_____

_____

_____

_____

_____

Reach high, for stars lie hidden in your soul.
Dream deep, for every dream precedes the goal.
PAMELA VAULL STARR

*Open wide the windows of our spirits and fill us full of light;
open wide the door of our hearts, that we may receive and
entertain Thee with all our powers of adoration.*
CHRISTINA ROSSETTI

Trust in the LORD with all thine heart;
and lean not unto thine own understanding.
In all thy ways acknowledge him, and he shall direct thy paths.
PROVERBS 3:5–6

Commit thy works unto the LORD,
and thy thoughts shall be established.

PROVERBS 16:3

_____

_____

_____

_____

_____

_____

_____

_____

_____

_____

_____

_____

_____

_____

_____

_____

_____

_____

_____

_____

_____

Everyone has a unique role to fill in the world and is important in some respect. Everyone, including and perhaps especially you, is indispensable.
NATHANIEL HAWTHORNE

Happiness is as a butterfly, which, when pursued, is always beyond your grasp, but which, if you will sit down quietly, may alight upon you.
NATHANIEL HAWTHORNE

Keep your face to the sunshine, and
you cannot see the shadow.
HELEN KELLER

We are what we repeatedly do.
Excellence, therefore, is not an act but a habit.

ARISTOTLE

_____

_____

_____

_____

_____

_____

_____

_____

_____

_____

_____

_____

_____

_____

_____

_____

_____

_____

_____

_____

No one is useless in this world who
lightens the burdens of it for another.
CHARLES DICKENS

You have achieved success if you have lived well, laughed often, and loved much.

ANONYMOUS

Today, well lived, makes every yesterday a dream
of happiness and every tomorrow a vision of hope.
SANSKRIT PROVERB

*Always be in a state of expectancy, and see that
you leave room for God to come in as He likes.*

OSWALD CHAMBERS

_____

_____

_____

_____

_____

_____

_____

_____

_____

_____

_____

_____

_____

_____

_____

_____

_____

_____

_____

Lead me in thy truth, and teach me: for thou art the God of my salvation;
on thee do I wait all the day.
PSALM 25:5

Now faith is the substance of things hoped for, the evidence of things not seen.

_____

_____

_____

_____

_____

_____

_____

_____

_____

_____

_____

_____

_____

_____

_____

_____

_____

_____

_____

A gentle word, a kind look, a good-natured smile can work wonders and accomplish miracles.
WILLIAM HAZLITT

*Let us learn to appreciate there will be times when the trees will be bare,
and look forward to the time when we may pick the fruit.*
ANTON CHEKHOV

_____

_____

_____

_____

_____

_____

_____

_____

_____

_____

_____

_____

_____

_____

_____

_____

_____

_____

_____

Twenty years from now, you will be more disappointed by the things that you didn't do than by the ones you did do. So throw off the bowlines. Sail away from the safe harbor. Catch the trade winds in your sails. Explore. Dream. Discover.

MARK TWAIN

_____

_____

_____

_____

_____

_____

_____

_____

_____

_____

_____

_____

_____

_____

_____

_____

_____

_____

_____

Life is to be fortified by many friendships.
To love and to be loved is the greatest happiness of existence.
SYDNEY SMITH

When things are complicated, I wish you simple beauty.
When things are chaotic, I wish you inner peace.
When things seem empty, I wish you hope and joy.
ANONYMOUS

_____

_____

_____

_____

_____

_____

_____

_____

_____

_____

_____

_____

_____

_____

_____

_____

_____

_____

_____

_____

Every great dream begins with a dreamer. Always remember, you have with you the strength, the patience, and the passion to reach for the stars to change the world.

HARRIET TUBMAN

Cherish your visions; cherish your ideals; cherish the music that stirs in your heart, the beauty that forms in your mind, the loveliness that drapes your purest thoughts, for out of them will grow all delightful conditions, all heavenly environment.

JAMES ALLEN

_____

_____

_____

_____

_____

_____

_____

_____

_____

_____

_____

_____

_____

_____

_____

_____

_____

_____

As we have therefore opportunity,
let us do good unto all men.
GALATIANS 6:10

*May our Lord Jesus Christ himself. . .
comfort your hearts, and stablish
you in every good word and work.*
THESSALONIANS 2:16–17

_____

_____

_____

_____

_____

_____

_____

_____

_____

_____

_____

_____

_____

_____

_____

_____

_____

_____

He turns not back who is bound to a star.
LEONARDO DA VINCI

Through many dangers, toils, and snares,
I have already come;
'Tis grace hath brought me safe thus far,
and grace will lead me home.

JOHN NEWTON

_____

_____

_____

_____

_____

_____

_____

_____

_____

_____

_____

_____

_____

_____

_____

_____

_____

_____

No act of kindness, no matter
how small, is ever wasted.
AESOP

All seasons are beautiful for the person who carries happiness within.
HORACE FRIESS

_____

_____

_____

_____

_____

_____

_____

_____

_____

_____

_____

_____

_____

_____

_____

_____

_____

_____

_____

_____

One way to get the most out of life
is to look upon it as an adventure.
WILLIAM FEATHER

Blessed is the influence of one true,
loving human soul on another.
GEORGE ELIOT

_____

_____

_____

_____

_____

_____

_____

_____

_____

_____

_____

_____

_____

_____

_____

_____

_____

_____

_____

_____

_____

_____

Prepare your mind to receive
the best that life has to offer.
ERNEST HOLMES

Let my soul take refuge. . .beneath the shadow of Your wings; let my heart, this sea of restless waves, find peace in You, O God.

ST. AUGUSTINE

_____

_____

_____

_____

_____

_____

_____

_____

_____

_____

_____

_____

_____

_____

_____

_____

_____

_____

_____

_____

Wherefore, if God so clothe the grass of the field,
which today is, and tomorrow is cast into the oven,
shall he not much more clothe you, O ye of little faith?

MATTHEW 6:30

*The eternal God is thy refuge,
and underneath are the everlasting arms.*
DEUTERONOMY 33:27

_____

_____

_____

_____

_____

_____

_____

_____

_____

_____

_____

_____

_____

_____

_____

_____

_____

_____

_____

_____

The creation of a thousand forests is in one acorn.
RALPH WALDO EMERSON

Grace turns lions into lambs, wolves into sheep,
monsters into men, and men into angels.
THOMAS CARLYLE

_____

_____

_____

_____

_____

_____

_____

_____

_____

_____

_____

_____

_____

_____

_____

_____

_____

_____

_____

_____

Keep your feet on the ground, but let your heart
soar as high as it will. Refuse to be average or
to surrender to the chill of your spiritual environment.
A. W. TOZER

Learn from yesterday, live for today, hope for tomorrow.

ALBERT EINSTEIN

_____

_____

_____

_____

_____

_____

_____

_____

_____

_____

_____

_____

_____

_____

_____

_____

_____

_____

_____

_____

_____

A kind heart is a fountain of gladness,
making everything in its vicinity freshen into smiles.
WASHINGTON IRVING

Success is not final; failure is not fatal:
It is the courage to continue that counts.
WINSTON CHURCHILL

_____

_____

_____

_____

_____

_____

_____

_____

_____

_____

_____

_____

_____

_____

_____

_____

_____

_____

_____

Do a deed of simple kindness;
Though its end you may not see,
It may reach, like widening ripples,
Down a long eternity.
JOSEPH PARKER NORRIS

Far away, there in the sunshine, are my highest aspirations. . . .
I can look up and see their beauty, believe in them,
and try to follow where they lead.

LOUISA MAY ALCOTT

_____

_____

_____

_____

_____

_____

_____

_____

_____

_____

_____

_____

_____

_____

_____

_____

_____

_____

_____

_____

Cast thy burden upon the LORD, and he shall sustain thee:
he shall never suffer the righteous to be moved.
PSALM 55:22

And it shall come to pass in the day that the LORD shall give thee rest from thy sorrow, and from thy fear, and from the hard bondage wherein thou wast made to serve.

ISAIAH 14:3

_Every person's life is a fairy
tale written by God's fingers._
HANS CHRISTIAN ANDERSEN

Patience and perseverance have a magical effect before which difficulties disappear and obstacles vanish.
JOHN QUINCY ADAMS

_____

_____

_____

_____

_____

_____

_____

_____

_____

_____

_____

_____

_____

_____

_____

_____

_____

_____

_____

_____

Knowledge is proud that it knows so much;
wisdom is humble that it knows no more.
WILLIAM COWPER

*One word frees us of all the weight
and pain of life: That word is love.*

SOPHOCLES

Each of us may be sure that if God sends us on stony paths,
He will provide us with strong shoes, and He will not send
us out on any journey for which He does not equip well.

ALEXANDER MACLAREN

Happiness makes up in height
for what it lacks in length.
ROBERT FROST

_____

_____

_____

_____

_____

_____

_____

_____

_____

_____

_____

_____

_____

_____

_____

_____

_____

_____

_____

_____

_____

_____

_____

_____

_____

_____

_____

_____

_____

_____

_____

_____

_____

_____

_____

_____

_____

*As each day comes to us refreshed and anew,
so does my gratitude renew itself daily. The
breaking of the sun over the horizon is my
grateful heart dawning upon a blessed world.*
ADABELLA RADICI

*I avoid looking forward or backward
and try to keep looking upward.*
CHARLOTTE BRONTË

_____

_____

_____

_____

_____

_____

_____

_____

_____

_____

_____

_____

_____

_____

_____

_____

_____

_____

_____

_____

Grace be with you, mercy, and peace, from God the Father,
and from the Lord Jesus Christ,
the Son of the Father, in truth and love.

2 JOHN 1:3

The LORD is gracious, and full of compassion;
slow to anger, and of great mercy.
PSALM 145:8

_____

_____

_____

_____

_____

_____

_____

_____

_____

_____

_____

_____

_____

_____

_____

_____

_____

_____

_____

The fountain of beauty is the heart, and every generous
thought illustrates the walls of your chamber.
FRANCIS QUARLES

Do all the good you can, by all the means you can,
in all the ways you can, in all the places you can,
at all the times you can, to all the people you can,
as long as ever you can.

JOHN WESLEY

This above all: To thine own self be true:
And it must follow as the night the day,
Thou canst not then be false to any man.
WILLIAM SHAKESPEARE

If you want happiness for an hour, take a nap.
If you want happiness for a day, go fishing.
If you want happiness for a year, inherit a fortune.
If you want happiness for a lifetime, help somebody.

CHINESE PROVERB

_____

_____

_____

_____

_____

_____

_____

_____

_____

_____

_____

_____

_____

_____

_____

_____

_____

_____

Humor is the great thing, the saving thing.
The minute it crops up, all our irritation and
resentment slip away, and a sunny spirit takes their place.
MARK TWAIN

The bluebird carries the sky on his back.
HENRY DAVID THOREAU

To succeed you need to find something to hold on to, something to motivate you, something to inspire you.
TONY DORSETT

*I want to help you to grow as beautiful as God
meant you to be when He thought of you first.*
GEORGE MACDONALD

_____

_____

_____

_____

_____

_____

_____

_____

_____

_____

_____

_____

_____

_____

_____

_____

_____

_____

_____

_____

My presence shall go with thee, and I will give thee rest.
EXODUS 33:14

Blessed be the God and Father of our Lord Jesus Christ,
who hath blessed us with all spiritual blessings in heavenly places in Christ.

EPHESIANS 1:3

_____

_____

_____

_____

_____

_____

_____

_____

_____

_____

_____

_____

_____

_____

_____

_____

_____

_____

_____

_____

The soul should always stand ajar,
ready to welcome the ecstatic experience.
EMILY DICKINSON

The grace of God is, in my mind, shaped like a key that comes from time to time and unlocks the heavy doors.

DONALD SWAN

_____

_____

_____

_____

_____

_____

_____

_____

_____

_____

_____

_____

_____

_____

_____

_____

_____

_____

_____

_____

Hope quickens all the still parts of
life and keeps the mind awake.
JOSEPH ADDISON

If God brings you to it,
He will bring you through it.

UNKNOWN

_____

_____

_____

_____

_____

_____

_____

_____

_____

_____

_____

_____

_____

_____

_____

_____

_____

_____

_____

*I am beginning to learn that it is the sweet,
simple things of life which are the real ones after all.*
LAURA INGALLS WILDER

The fragrance always stays in
the hand that gives the rose.

HADA BEJAR

_____

_____

_____

_____

_____

_____

_____

_____

_____

_____

_____

_____

_____

_____

_____

_____

_____

_____

_____

_____

_____

Let us not be content to wait and see what will happen,
but give us the determination to make the right things happen.

HORACE MANN

Let there be many windows to your soul,
that all the glory of the universe may beautify it.
ELLA WHEELER WILCOX

_____

_____

_____

_____

_____

_____

_____

_____

_____

_____

_____

_____

_____

_____

_____

_____

_____

_____

_____

It is of the LORD's mercies that we are not consumed, because his compassions fail not. They are new every morning: great is thy faithfulness.

LAMENTATIONS 3:22–23

That Christ may dwell in your hearts by faith;
that ye, being rooted and grounded in love.

EPHESIANS 3:17

_____

_____

_____

_____

_____

_____

_____

_____

_____

_____

_____

_____

_____

_____

_____

_____

_____

_____

_____

_____

Your only treasures are those
which you carry in your heart.
DEMOPHILUS

Every day is an opportunity to
make a new happy ending.
UNKNOWN

_____

_____

_____

_____

_____

_____

_____

_____

_____

_____

_____

_____

_____

_____

_____

_____

_____

_____

_____

_____

By perseverance the snail reached the ark.
CHARLES SPURGEON

*Contentment is not the fulfillment of what you want
but the realization of how much you already have.*

ANONYMOUS

_____

_____

_____

_____

_____

_____

_____

_____

_____

_____

_____

_____

_____

_____

_____

_____

_____

_____

Be glad of life, because it gives you the chance to love,
to work, to play, and to look up at the stars.
HENRY VAN DYKE

True silence is the rest of the mind; it is to the spirit what sleep is to the body—nourishment and refreshment.

WILLIAM PENN

_____

_____

_____

_____

_____

_____

_____

_____

_____

_____

_____

_____

_____

_____

_____

_____

_____

_____

_____

_____

We are the most appealing to others, and happiest within,
when we are completely ourselves.
LUCI SWINDOLL

Nothing is so strong as gentleness,
and nothing so gentle as real strength.
FRANCIS DE SALES

Peace I leave with you, my peace I give unto you:
not as the world giveth, give I unto you.
Let not your heart be troubled, neither let it be afraid.

JOHN 14:27

Thy mercy, O LORD, is in the heavens; and thy faithfulness reacheth unto the clouds. Thy righteousness is like the great mountains; thy judgments are a great deep: O LORD, thou preservest man and beast.

PSALM 36:5–6

_____

_____

_____

_____

_____

_____

_____

_____

_____

_____

_____

_____

_____

_____

_____

_____

_____

_____

It isn't the great big pleasures that count the most;
it's making a great deal out of the little ones.
JEAN WEBSTER

Love is the divine vitality that everywhere produces and restores life.
To each and every one of us, it gives the power of working miracles.

LYDIA MARIA CHILD

_____

_____

_____

_____

_____

_____

_____

_____

_____

_____

_____

_____

_____

_____

_____

_____

_____

_____

*Each dawn holds a new hope for a new plan,
making the start of each day the start of a new life.*
GINA BLAIR

*Cheerfulness and contentment are great beautifiers
and are famous preservers of youthful looks.*
CHARLES DICKENS

_____

_____

_____

_____

_____

_____

_____

_____

_____

_____

_____

_____

_____

_____

_____

_____

_____

_____

_____

_____

To accomplish great things, we must not only
act but also dream, not only plan but also believe.
ANATOLE FRANCE

To me, a lush carpet of pine needles or spongy grass is more welcome than the most luxurious Persian rug.

HELEN KELLER

_____

_____

_____

_____

_____

_____

_____

_____

_____

_____

_____

_____

_____

_____

_____

_____

_____

_____

_____

_He does most in God's great world who
does his best in his own little world._

THOMAS JEFFERSON

Where others see but the dawn coming over the hill,
I see the soul of God shouting for joy.
WILLIAM BLAKE

_____

_____

_____

_____

_____

_____

_____

_____

_____

_____

_____

_____

_____

_____

_____

_____

_____

_____

_____

He doeth great things and unsearchable;
marvellous things without number.

JOB 5:9

The mercy of the LORD is from everlasting to everlasting upon them that fear him, and his righteousness unto children's children.

PSALM 103:17

_____

_____

_____

_____

_____

_____

_____

_____

_____

_____

_____

_____

_____

_____

_____

_____

_____

_____

_____

_____

The glory is not in never failing
but in rising every time you fail.
CHINESE PROVERB

Live as if you were to die tomorrow.
Learn as if you were to live forever.
MAHATMA GANDHI

_____

_____

_____

_____

_____

_____

_____

_____

_____

_____

_____

_____

_____

_____

_____

_____

_____

_____

_____

_____

_____

We need time to dream, time to remember,
and time to reach the infinite. Time to be.
GLADYS TABER

*The happiness of life is made up of minute fractions—
the little, soon-forgotten charities of a kiss or a smile,
a kind look or a heartfelt compliment.*

SAMUEL TAYLOR COLERIDGE

_____
_____
_____
_____
_____
_____
_____
_____
_____
_____
_____
_____
_____
_____
_____
_____
_____
_____
_____

Happiness held is the seed;
happiness shared is the flower.
UNKNOWN

Live your life while you have it. Life is a splendid gift.
There is nothing small about it.

FLORENCE NIGHTINGALE

_____

_____

_____

_____

_____

_____

_____

_____

_____

_____

_____

_____

_____

_____

_____

_____

_____

_____

_____

This is the miracle that happens every time to those who really love; the more they give, the more they possess.
RAINER MARIA RILKE

The splendor of the rose and the whiteness of the lily do not rob the little violet of its scent nor the daisy of its simple charm. If every tiny flower wanted to be a rose, spring would lose its loveliness.

THÉRÈSE OF LISIEUX

_____

_____

_____

_____

_____

_____

_____

_____

_____

_____

_____

_____

_____

_____

_____

_____

_____

_____

And the LORD shall guide thee continually, and satisfy thy soul in drought, and make fat thy bones: and thou shalt be like a watered garden, and like a spring of water, whose waters fail not.
ISAIAH 58:11

I will cause the shower to come down in his season;
there shall be showers of blessing.
EZEKIEL 34:26

_____

_____

_____

_____

_____

_____

_____

_____

_____

_____

_____

_____

_____

_____

_____

_____

_____

_____

_____

The greatest use of life is to spend it
for something that will outlast it.
WILLIAM JAMES

The great things are so simple;
the simple are so great!
FRED G. BOWLES

_____

_____

_____

_____

_____

_____

_____

_____

_____

_____

_____

_____

_____

_____

_____

_____

_____

_____

_____

_____

*When we take time to notice the simple things in life,
we never lack for encouragement. We discover we are
surrounded by limitless hope that's just wearing everyday clothes.*
ANONYMOUS

Kind words can be short and easy to speak,
but their echoes are truly endless.
MOTHER TERESA

_____

_____

_____

_____

_____

_____

_____

_____

_____

_____

_____

_____

_____

_____

_____

_____

_____

_____

_____

_____

_____

Hold a hand that needs you
and discover abundant joy.
FLAVIA WEEDN

The heart that loves is always young.
GREEK PROVERB

We are made to reach out beyond our grasp.
OSWALD CHAMERS

The joyful birds prolong the strain, their song with every spring renewed;
the air we breathe, and falling rain, each softly whispers: God is good.

JOHN HAMPDEN GURNEY

_____

_____

_____

_____

_____

_____

_____

_____

_____

_____

_____

_____

_____

_____

_____

_____

_____

_____

And God is able to make all grace abound toward you; that ye, always having all sufficiency in all things, may abound to every good work.

2 CORINTHIANS 9:8

He shall feed his flock like a shepherd: he shall gather the lambs with his arm, and carry them in his bosom, and shall gently lead those that are with young.

ISAIAH 40:11

_____

_____

_____

_____

_____

_____

_____

_____

_____

_____

_____

_____

_____

_____

_____

_____

_____

_____

Happiness is a sunbeam. . . . *When it strikes a kindred heart, like the converged lights upon a mirror, it reflects itself with redoubled brightness. It is not perfected until it is shared.*
JANE PORTER

Optimism is the faith that leads to achievement.
Nothing can be done without hope and confidence.

HELEN KELLER

_____

_____

_____

_____

_____

_____

_____

_____

_____

_____

_____

_____

_____

_____

_____

_____

_____

_____

_____

God has given us two hands—one to receive with and the other to give with. We are not cisterns made for hoarding; we are channels made for sharing.
BILLY GRAHAM

Life is like a mirror—we get the best results when we smile at it.

ANONYMOUS

_____

_____

_____

_____

_____

_____

_____

_____

_____

_____

_____

_____

_____

_____

_____

_____

_____

_____

_____

_____

Mix a little foolishness with your serious plans.
It is lovely to be silly at the right moment.
HORACE

Forget not that the earth delights to feel your bare feet and the winds long to play with your hair.
KAHLIL GIBRAN

_____

_____

_____

_____

_____

_____

_____

_____

_____

_____

_____

_____

_____

_____

_____

_____

_____

_____

_____

_____

I often think flowers are the angels' alphabet, whereby they write on hills and fields mysterious and beautiful lessons for us to feel and learn.

LOUISA MAY ALCOTT

Lovely flowers are the smiles of God's goodness.
WILLIAM WILBERFORCE

_____

_____

_____

_____

_____

_____

_____

_____

_____

_____

_____

_____

_____

_____

_____

_____

_____

_____

_____

_____

No man hath seen God at any time. If we love one another, God dwelleth in us, and his love is perfected in us.
1 JOHN 4:12

Greater love hath no man than this,
that a man lay down his life for his friends.

JOHN 15:13

_____

_____

_____

_____

_____

_____

_____

_____

_____

_____

_____

_____

_____

_____

_____

_____

_____

_____

_____

Your world is as big as you make it.
GEORGIA DOUGLAS JOHNSON

*He who distributes the milk of human kindness
cannot help but spill a little on himself.*

JAMES M. BARRIE

_____

_____

_____

_____

_____

_____

_____

_____

_____

_____

_____

_____

_____

_____

_____

_____

_____

_____

_____

Let us be grateful to people who make us happy;
they are the charming gardeners who make our souls blossom.
MARCEL PROUST

*Within each of us, just waiting to blossom,
is the wonderful promise of all we can be.*
ANONYMOUS

_____

_____

_____

_____

_____

_____

_____

_____

_____

_____

_____

_____

_____

_____

_____

_____

_____

_____

_____

Plunge boldly into the thick of life,
and seize it where you will; it is always interesting.
JOHANN WOLFGANG VON GOETHE

Life is a flower of which love is the honey.
VICTOR HUGO

How wonderful it is that nobody need wait a single moment before starting to improve the world.
ANNE FRANK

Give thanks for unknown blessings already on their way.
NATIVE AMERICAN PROVERB

_____

_____

_____

_____

_____

_____

_____

_____

_____

_____

_____

_____

_____

_____

_____

_____

_____

_____

_____

_____

Behold, what manner of love the Father hath bestowed upon us,
that we should be called the sons of God.
1 JOHN 3:1

Know therefore that the LORD thy God, he is God, the faithful God, which keepeth covenant and mercy with them that love him and keep his commandments to a thousand generations.

DEUTERONOMY 7:9

There never was any heart truly great and generous
that was not also tender and compassionate.
ROBERT SOUTH

The voyage of discovery is not in seeking new landscapes but in having new eyes.
MARCEL PROUST

Kindness in words creates confidence.
Kindness in thinking creates profoundness.
Kindness in giving creates love.
LAO TZU

Life is so full of meaning and purpose, so full of beauty,
beneath its covering, that you will find that
earth but cloaks your heaven.

FRA GIOVANNI GIOCONDO

_____

_____

_____

_____

_____

_____

_____

_____

_____

_____

_____

_____

_____

_____

_____

_____

_____

_____

_____

_____

_____

In everyone's life, at some time, our inner fire goes out.
It is then burst into flame by an encounter with another human being.
We should all be thankful for those people who rekindle the inner spirit.
ALBERT SCHWEITZER

The riches that are in the
heart cannot be stolen.
RUSSIAN PROVERB

Let us not hurry so in our pace of living
that we lose sight of the art of living.
FRANCIS BACON

For we are his workmanship, created in Christ Jesus unto good works,
which God hath before ordained that we should walk in them.

EPHESIANS 2:1